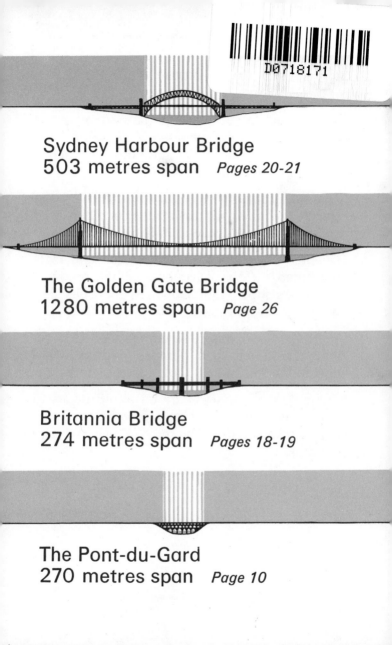

Sydney Harbour Bridge
503 metres span *Pages 20-21*

The Golden Gate Bridge
1280 metres span *Page 26*

Britannia Bridge
274 metres span *Pages 18-19*

The Pont-du-Gard
270 metres span *Page 10*

to teachers and parents

This is a LADYBIRD LEADER book, one of a series specially produced to meet the very real need for carefully planned *first information books* that instantly attract enquiring minds and stimulate reluctant readers.

The subject matter and vocabulary have been selected with expert assistance, and the brief and simple text is printed in large, clear type.

Children's questions are anticipated and facts presented in a logical sequence. Where possible, the books show what happened in the past and what is relevant today.

Special artwork has been commissioned to set a standard rarely seen in books for this reading age and at this price.

Full colour illustrations are on all 48 pages to give maximum impact and provide the extra enrichment that is the aim of all Ladybird Leaders.

A Ladybird Leader

bridges

written by Robert Loxley
illustrated by Gerald Witcomb and Gavin Rowe

Ladybird Books Ltd Loughborough 1976

Nature made the first bridges

The very first bridges
were not made by men.

Fallen trees were used to cross rivers.

Trees used like this
were simple 'beam' bridges.

A beam bridge over a road

In hot countries,
ropes were made from vine stems.

The ends were tied to trees
to make the first 'suspension' bridges.

A suspension
bridge

Another natural crossing

Some shallow rivers have rocks in them.
People crossed
by stepping from stone to stone.
In some rivers, broad flat stones
were put down as 'stepping stones'.

A simple stone bridge

Later, piles of stones
were placed in a river.

Flat stone slabs were put across them.

These made a 'clapper' bridge.

The first arches

Falls of rock
sometimes make
a natural arched bridge.

Stone slabs can break
if they are too long.

Men learned how to make an arch
with smaller stones.

A stone bridge is stronger with an arch.

A Roman bridge that is still used

The Romans were great bridge builders.

The Roman who built this one said,
'I will build a bridge
that will last for ever!'

A Roman bridge
at Alcantara, Spain.

9

A tall Roman bridge with many arches

The Pont-du-Gard,
Nîmes, France.

If a valley was very deep,
the Romans built arches
on top of other arches.

The Roman word for water was
'aqua' (ak-wa).

This bridge carried water to a town,
so it is called an aqueduct.

A stone bridge of the Middle Ages

The pointed 'cutwaters' of this bridge stop the stonework being worn away.

Long ago, people stood in the 'refuges' out of the way of horses and carts.

These refuges are still useful today.

A packhorse bridge of the 17th century

When there were few roads,
goods were often carried in packs
on the backs of horses or mules.

The bridges built for them
were called packhorse bridges.

A very tall stone bridge

Bridges with arches can be very tall.
This one is in Switzerland.
It carries a railway
over a very deep valley.

Landwasser Viaduct,
Switzerland.

A bridge made of wood

This wooden bridge is in Africa.
It is called a 'trestle' bridge.
Many bridges like this were built
to carry the first railways in America.

How 'braces' make a bridge stronger

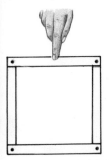

*If pressed straight down,
this frame is quite strong*

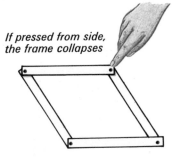

*If pressed from side,
the frame collapses*

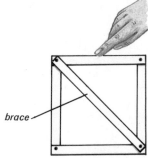

brace

*The brace keeps
the frame firm.*

The first iron bridge

The first bridge made of iron
was built in Shropshire (Salop),
England in 1779.

The place became known as Ironbridge.

Before that time,
bridges had been made
of rope, stone, brick or wood.

A bridge of iron tubes

The Britannia Bridge
is a beam bridge.

A railway runs
through its iron tubes.

The tubes were floated from the shore.
Then they were lifted into place
over 30 metres
above the water.

Britannia Bridge,
Menai Strait,
North Wales.

A famous steel bridge in Australia

Sydney Harbour Bridge
has the largest steel arch in the world.

The bridge has eight traffic lanes,
two railway lines, a footway
and a bicycle track.

How the bridge was built

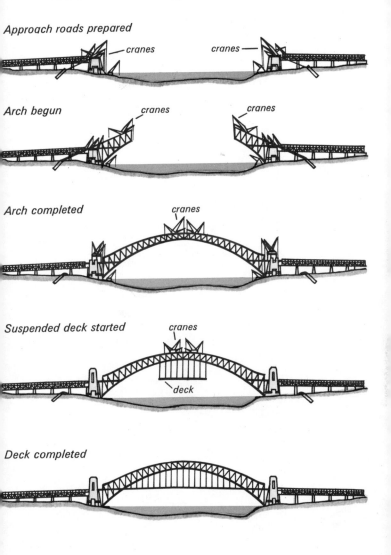

Approach roads prepared

cranes — cranes

Arch begun

cranes — cranes

Arch completed

cranes

Suspended deck started

cranes

deck

Deck completed

A modern bridge with a concrete arch

The Gladesville Bridge is also at Sydney.
It is a very fine, modern bridge.
Steel rods in the concrete
give it extra strength.

This simple bridge is weak

An arch gives strength

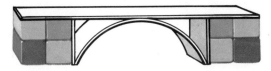

Arch added to bridge

Bridge is now stronger

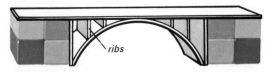

ribs

Ribs make bridge stronger still

Try making a bridge like this with cardboard

A steel suspension bridge

The roadway of this bridge
is hung (suspended) on steel cables.

It was built by
Isambard Kingdom Brunel,
a great British engineer.

In a gale, the middle of the bridge
can move 300 mm up and down.

Clifton Suspension Bridge
at Bristol, England.

How a suspension bridge must be supported

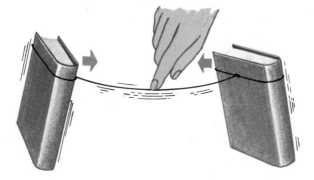

When the middle of the string is pressed, the books fall inwards

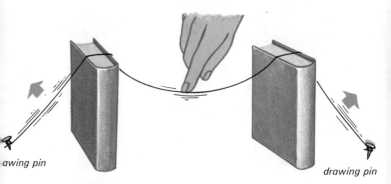

drawing pin

drawing pin

With the ends of the string fastened like this, the books will not fall inwards

Some modern steel suspension bridges

The roadway of this bridge
is 81 metres above the water.
It is called the Golden Gate Bridge
because ships leaving the bay
in the evening sail into the sunset.

The Golden Gate
Suspension Bridge,
San Francisco.

This bridge carries a road
that joins England to Wales.

It crosses the River Severn
where it is 1.6 kilometres wide.

Drivers pay to use the bridge.

This helps to pay the building cost.

The Severn Bridge
near Bristol, England.

The Forth Railway Bridge

A bridge like this
is called a cantilever bridge.
This one is a railway bridge in Scotland.

It took seven years to build.
Some of the steel tubes you see
are as wide as the tunnels
of the London Underground Railway.

Bricks resting
on the ground

The lower picture shows how the load is spread over a cantilever bridge.

A cantilever bridge.

Bricks resting on the ground

The girl's weight is easily supported.

A concrete road bridge

Many concrete road bridges
have been built in modern times.

Even the Romans
knew about concrete.

They sometimes used it.

A concrete road bridge
in France.

A very unusual bridge

The Chesapeake Bay Bridge
is 28.2 kilometres long.

Part of it is a cantilever bridge,
part a suspension bridge
and part a trestle bridge.

The Chesapeake Bay Bridge
in America.

A bridge that moves up and down

The roadway of London's Tower Bridge can move up to let ships pass through.

Often, small wooden canal bridges lift up to let boats through.

Bridges that swing round

Here is another way
of letting ships pass a bridge.

The Barton
swing bridges,
Lancashire,
England.

Both these bridges turn
from the middle.

One is part of a canal.

The other carries a road.

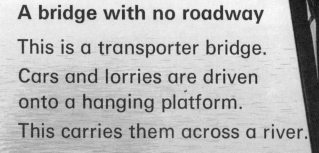

A bridge with no roadway

This is a transporter bridge.
Cars and lorries are driven
onto a hanging platform.
This carries them across a river.

An old fortified bridge

Long ago, some bridges were fortified
to stop an enemy crossing them.

Molten lead and boiling oil
were dropped from this tower
onto attackers.

Monnow Bridge,
Monmouth, Wales.

Bridges in wartime

Bridges are still important targets
in wartime.
Aircraft have destroyed many like this
in modern wars.

Pontoon bridges

The Romans used 'pontoon' bridges.
Modern armies still use them.
Flat-bottomed boats hold up
the roadway of this pontoon bridge.

Mobile bridges

Today, an army can soon bridge a river.
Special carriers move bridges like this
into position, even under enemy fire.

Old London Bridge

In 1666, London Bridge looked like this.

On it there were shops, houses,
a chapel and a drawbridge.

Many of the buildings were burned down
in the Great Fire of London.

Old London Bridge was pulled down
in 1831.

A new bridge had been built by then.

It was twice as wide
and took seven years to build.

A bridge to give pleasure

Bridges like this were sometimes made
to be looked at, rather than to be used.

They were built by rich people
in the parks round their homes.

They were part of a view
seen from a big house.

A bridge of sadness

Once prisoners crossed this bridge
from a palace to a prison in Venice.

There they were put to death.

It is known as 'The Bridge of Sighs'.

Bridges with houses

Houses were built on some old bridges.

The rent from the houses
helped to pay for the bridge.

The houses on this bridge
were built in 1540.

Lincoln High Bridge, England.

At Ambleside, in England's Lake District,
this charming little house
stands alone on its small bridge.

It was built about 200 years ago.

A great bridge disaster

In a gale, on a Sunday in 1879,
part of this bridge fell into the water.

A railway train fell with it
and 80 people were killed.

The Tay Bridge, Scotland,
December 1879.

Page 9
A stone arch bridge
A Roman bridge across the Tagus, Alcantara, Spain

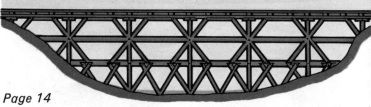

Page 14
A timber trestle bridge

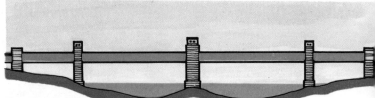

Pages 18-19
A beam bridge
Britannia Bridge over the Menai Strait, Wales

Page 34
A movement (or bascule) bridge
Tower Bridge, London

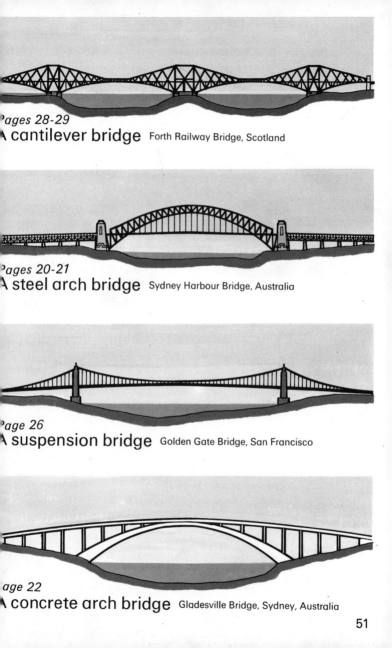

A cantilever bridge Forth Railway Bridge, Scotland

A steel arch bridge Sydney Harbour Bridge, Australia

A suspension bridge Golden Gate Bridge, San Francisco

A concrete arch bridge Gladesville Bridge, Sydney, Australia

Index